HIS
SPOKEN
WORD

In Lyrics & Poetry

Gail Marie King

His Spoken Word: In Lyrics & Poetry
Gail Marie King

Ebook ISBN: 978-1-7370914-1-7
Print ISBN: 978-1-7370914-9-3

Published by Gail Marie King
P.O. Box 146766
Chicago, IL 60614-8553
GailKing.com

Unless otherwise indicated, all Scripture quotations are taken from the King James Version (KJV) of the Bible.

Amplified Bible (AMP)
Copyright © 2015 by The Lockman Foundation, La Habra, CA 90631. All rights reserved.

This book is dedicated to my beloved Jesus Christ, my loving family, and every believer. May every creative soul be edified.

In the beginning [before all time] was the Word (Christ), and the Word was with God, and the Word was God Himself.

— JOHN 1:1, AMP

CONTENTS

Introduction

Ten years ago, in a single night, most of this book poured forth. I give glory to God's Holy Spirit for allowing a girl who grew up in the Ida B. Wells Projects of Chicago to survive and thrive. Our cultural experiences of poverty, crime, and fatherlessness have a voice. This voice has turned to song, poetry, hip hop, jazz, and more.

The Lord is calling all His sons and daughters to take our places in His Kingdom—on earth. He has confirmed our diverse gifts and has allowed us to show up with a *divine message*.

I pray that these words will lift a head and a heart, and support awareness. We continue through *His Spoken Word!*

— *Gail Marie King*

Ode to J. Lindsey

This is a subject
I feel passionate about.
It's so important
to get this message out.

When I was a teen,
Auntie came to me
and said, "James is not your father,
it was a trick, you see."

I turned to Mama
for verification,
but she didn't deny
this altercation.

So, where's the man
that's my real dad?
How can I find him,
and who is he?

My paradigm shifted…
What did he look like?
Who is the one?
Will I ever meet him?
Will that day ever come?

The pain cuts deep.
I could not understand.
Wasn't I *worth* it?
He just *ran*?

But a force inside said,
"You're not through,
God has a future for you."

Now when I see
a man walking out,
on a little baby…
it angers me.
You could have the baby tested,
if he's a *maybe*.

They said, "He left your mother
while she was pregnant with you.
He's already married.
He was scared,
so he flew!"

His last name is Lindsey.
They gave me that.
Does that make me
an unwanted, illegitimate brat?

The brief history of
my biological dad
wounded me bad.
He left me to grow up
in the slum—poor, rejected,
and mad.

Unknowingly,
he crushed an innocent baby girl
and distorted my world.
Why was I dating older men?
Are they filling in for *him*?

Again, that force said,
"You're not through;
God is with you."

One day,
I ran to a church.
I needed to be healed
of the men who hurt me
and the hand I'd been dealt.

When a parent walks away,
it wounds to the bone.
But God kept whispering,
"I'm your father,
in *Me*, you have a home."

Listen, single men,
don't take the bait.
Find out for sure,
if it's *your* baby—*don't wait!*

Sometimes, the mama
don't really know who.
So they come with a lawsuit
and sue *you.*

It's OK,
get the DNA test *today.*
The mom should see your side.
If it's truly *your* baby …
what's there to hide?

Remember, none of us is through.
God has a plan for you.
Now you have a reason.
It's your season.
Go ahead, be a man.
Bless your children.

Don't dodge the truth.
You're not escaping.
God will demand an answer,
concerning that tiny face.

What were you thinking?
Fathers, mothers,
it's a new day.
We've got to love and protect
all flesh.
It's the only way.
The world has turned its back.
We don't love babies, children, or teens.

Crime has catapulted,
as this generation grows up
lonely, displaced, and mean.

But you're not through.
God is love, and He wants *you.*

Men, what do you do now?
You got kids out there...
and you're running for cover.
All the time,
on the prowl,
for another new lover.

It's not too late.
Stop the madness.
End the strife.
Stop sleeping with *fast girls*
you *know* will never be a wife!

You say, "Everyone's doing it."
What excuse is that?
Everyone's *not* doing it,
and that's a statistical fact.
Anyone with a future
avoids that path.
Check the facts.

Be wise, my loving brother.
Stop sleeping around.
It's a bad example
and will *keep you down.*

Remain at peace
with your baby's mother.
You created a life,
and you'll need each other.

Insist on advanced training.
You'll perish without knowledge.
Find your children.
Make knowing the Lord
their first college.

Son, you're not through.
Start anew.
God is love,
and He's waiting patiently
to help *you*.
Allow Him
to transform your world.
Let *the Lord* support you!

Elohim

In the shadows, we hid,
condemned,
sold into slavery, and sin.

But Jehovah Tsidkenu,
the Lord our Righteousness,
the High Priest & Apostle,
the Head of the Church,
set us free.

The Man of Sorrows said,
"Come, find refuge in Me."
The weight of
guilt and shame
crushed our Spirit
and ruined our names.

But Jehovah Mekoddishkem,
the Lord our Sanctifier,
stepped up
and baptized us
in His blood.

In the river of living water,
the Holy One Himself,
our judge and ruler,
washed our bodies and spirits
within His holiness.

As a people, we were
too tired to go on.
But Jehovah Shalom,
the Lord our Peace,
our hope,
the image of the invisible God,
laid our weary heads on His shoulder.
Jah alone
carried us home.

When we didn't know,
how we would eat,
sleep, or live.
Jehovah Jireh,
the Lord our Provider,
anointed someone to step in.
The Bread of Life,
it is He
that fed us.

Like a dragon,
fear ruled us.
But the Lion of the Tribe of Judah,
Jehovah Nissi,
the Lord our Banner
Jehovah Sabaoth,
the Lord of Armies
El Rohi,
the Lord, our Shepherd,
guarded and protected us.

Yah exposed every deception,
He rebuked the enemy.
The carpenter rebuilt us
as His temple.
Pain, sickness,
and even death tormented.

But Jehovah Rapha,
the Lord, our Healer,
renewed our strength
and restored our souls.

We mounted up
on wings like eagles.
We ran and were not weary;
we walked and were not faint.

Some perished for lack of knowledge,
not knowing what to do
or where to turn.
But the Master, Yahshua,
the Wisdom of God,
the Wonderful Counselor,
our Eternal Father,
our Bright Morning Star,
the Light of the World,
brought us through.
The Chief Cornerstone
is our maker.

El Yisrael, Yahweh,
the God of Israel,
He said,
"Lean not unto your own understanding,
in all your ways acknowledge Me,
I AM will direct your path."

They say we are all alone,
But Jehovah Shammah,
the Lord is here.
Emmanuel the Lord
is with us.
The King of Kings
and Lord of Lords
said,
"I will never leave you
or forsake you."

Adonai,
the Lord our Great God,
loves us.

Jehovah Shammah,
our Companion is here.
The Bright Morning Star
has kissed us.

The Prince of Peace
lovingly caresses us.
Even though no one else
accepted us.
The Chosen One,
our Hope,
our Beloved Bridegroom has declared,
"You are Mine."

When there was no one to trust,
because man is but dust,
Jehovah,
Faithful and True,
led the way,
sharing life and truth.

Yah,
the Lord Who Never Changes,
the True Vine,
the Son of God said,
"Come live in the shelter of the Most High,
find rest in the shadow of the Almighty,
I alone will be your refuge,
your place of safety."

Yah,
He is our God,
and we trust Him.

Prodigal Son

Lord, I'm sorry,
for the way I treated Mama.
She gave all she had but left here *sad*.

You said to honor your father
and honor your mother.
Forgive me, Lord.
I really do love her.

What was wrong with me?
I don't understand.
Heal me, Jesus.
Take my hands.

Mama, wherever you are,
this is your son,
loving you from afar.
I'm down on my knees,
...forgive me, *please*.

Lord, lift Mama so she can dance.
Let me love her.
Give us another chance.

You gave me a queen,
but I was so mean.
She was sent from your throne,
but in my rebellion,
I couldn't see who she was.

Now I come before God,
repenting this day,
wash me in the blood
and show me the way.

Mama wasn't perfect,
but I vow to love.
Things sometimes go wrong,
but family—
we got *each other*.

Lord, you said, "Honor
your father
and honor your mother,
love her,
and your days will be long."

Love Never Fails

It's easy to love Jesus,
He's humble and kind.
He loves everyone, despite color, behavior,
or state of mind.

Just think,
God Himself came to earth.
He allowed mere men
to spit in his face,
as an example
for us.

He endured disrespect, offense,
discomfort, and threats.
Finally, they murdered Him.
But He *paid* sin's debt.

Now every man is freed,
as he believes
in Jesus.

He opens our hearts to see,
but we must relinquish sin,
selfishness, and greed.

The Almighty was brought low.
And He commanded us,
"Come,
pick up your cross,
and follow."

Why is there
so much strife,
in marriage, family,
on the job,
in life?

Are we missing the Lord
and void of His Word?
Have we fallen for the lie?
Fights are not about *who* is right.
They challenge us
to see through *His* eyes.

We say we are searching
for *true love.*
But if that's true,
why must everyone
serve *us?*

Love gives and gives,
both money and time.
It never demands,
"Where's mine?"

Joy is fleeting to those who keep score.
Why become bitter,
demanding—*more and more!*

We yearn for a love
where we don't pay or perform.
Thank you, Jesus, I've found it!
It's called *the love of God*.

Have faith in His Word,
not news and views.
Love unconditionally.
I promise
you won't lose.

Jesus,
You are so easy to love.
Heal my heart
toward my brothers.

Help me free myself
from demanding
so much of others.

There's a line between
standing up for right
and living filled with anger
to justify hate.

Very few know it,
but offense
is poisonous bait.
Don't take it!

Lean on the Lord
and wait.
You'll see your enemies
fall away.

I've come to Jesus.
He's healed my heart.
It's OK to cry.
Leave it behind
and make a new start.

I release all the anger,
the hurt,
the memories,
the pain.

I understand
that the price was paid
when Christ was slain.

It's invigorating
to love unconditionally,
enjoying sisters and brothers
with no secret agenda.

God's love is immense!
And the secret is this...
it's available to everyone
who *refuses* offense.

You're mine,
I'm yours,
and we are His.

Wake Up

How can we let these atrocities go on?
Don't you believe Jesus?
He's coming home.
Wake up and live.
Love, pitch in, and give.

The whole world has been sold a lie.
We are not separated from those who died.
It's not true.
Pay attention to what *you* do.

We are responsible for kids in Africa
and the homeless man sleeping on
North Michigan Avenue.
Addicts are suffering in every mecca
while millions of seniors are forgotten, too.

How did we become so callous?
Death has become another source of entertainment.
We indulge every form of malice, anything
that will command a dollar.

We said a change is coming.
That's a bit late.
The change has already come,
according to events to date.

The greedy are falling fast.
The violent don't last.
Where we see hope
is where we see growth.

God, put a dream in our hearts.
Dust them off.
Help families and communities
to make a new start.
Publish that book.

There's a war going on,
strap on your gear!
Want to live?
Wake up, forgive, pitch in.
Jesus said,
"If you did it for them,
you did it for Me."

I Forgive You, I Forgive Me

Examine this life
we've been blessed to live.
Why did Christ stress?
"Let it go. F*orgive*."

Did I *hurt myself* when I demanded of you,
what you didn't possess?

You said something I didn't like.
You did something I didn't approve of.
But I'm not your God.
Who am I to judge you?

I have no idea,
what you are going through.

I do know that Jesus said,
"You must forgive others,
because God has forgiven you."

It's easy for me
to blame *you* for my pain,
rather than face the truth.

You're not responsible
for how I feel.
It's up to me to mature,
to grow and to heal.

Jesus, help me to forgive.
I release the prisoners
from my self-imposed hell.

Lord, help me
to stop blaming others
for not being what I need.
I can love them as they are
and go where *You* lead.

Thank you, Jesus!
Your blood cleansed my heart.
I'm free to love everyone
just as they are.

As I remember the past,
I breathe a sigh of release.
I'm so grateful to God
for the life of Jesus!

In you Lord,
I've found joy and peace.
How freeing!
I quickly pronounce,
to anyone who offends,
I forgive you,
and I forgive me!

It's a Rap!

Here's another wolf,
posing as a lamb
to seduce me.

I went to God, praying,
"Lord, please loose me!"

I've learned
doing what is right
is the shortcut.
You can't convince me otherwise,
no ifs, ands, or butts.

He said,
"I will be found by all who seek Me."
So, I touched His robe,
and He healed me.

I no longer sit
on any barstool,
just doesn't make sense.
I *stay* lit from within.

My prayer is for you
to find the peace
that will pull you through.
Jehovah Shalom
is waiting for you, too.

This new life
Christ has promised
is full of joy,
minus the drama.

Dust off your dreams
and put away schemes.
All you need
is a clean heart.
Go ahead,
make a new start.

Our Lord will take the lead,
restoring love, sending help
and *everything* you will need.

It's a rap!

This Violence Must Stop

What must we do
to get the message through?

This violence must stop!
It's not OK
to blow a brother away.

We can celebrate life
and do each other right.
We're all on this hill.
Let's not kill.
We were made to cherish,
not perish.

Never hit a female
when we can walk out.
Don't go to jail,
why die young?
What about our sons?

Pass the word,
self-hatred is absurd!
God has come,
He's shaking us,
one by one.
This violence *must* stop!

Lord, Thank You

Jesus gave us this new life,
absent of strife.
Lord, thank you for saving me!

And when we didn't have a dime,
He paid the bills on time.
They say we're crazy,
but it's joy in you and me.

We released sin
and running with loose men.
You've given us light.
Hallelujah!
We're finally living right.

We're not searching for a hunk
or living in a funk
and drunk.
We love everyone,
we fellowship,
we have fun.

My past
is out of sight,
and the future is bright
full of His light.
We will walk in your way
each and every day.

Since the day we repented,
our lives make sense.
We have no shame,
how we praise Your name!
Lord, thank you for saving me!

Shelter

Found myself
in another jam.

I cried,
Lord,
help me out.

You said,
"Come boldly
before My throne."

Why do I fear
stumbling,
lost and alone?

I thirst for
your godly advice
and a miracle
to overcome enemies
and strife.

I praise you, Lord,
for who you are.
I lay down sense knowledge,
pride, and vainglory.

Your wisdom
is like the finest of wine,
your calming touch
forever mine.
Your love
unfathomable,
your ways
insurmountable.

Be my first,
and my last.
I worship you, Lord,
releasing
my fallen past.

Love Guaranteed

Hey, young girl,
with those pretty curls,
smelling good,
and strolling through the hood …

One day, you'll see,
in Jesus, you're rich.
His love is guaranteed;
everything you need
is within reach.

What's it all about?
Do you even know?
You're running fast,
developing a past.

We got all this "cute"
but no loot.
Let's wake up.
Nobody gives a hoot.
Be smart.
Ditch that brute!

You're not for sale,
save your soul,
skip jail…and the hell.

Hey, Miss Cute,
with no loot,
get a clue.
He's not into you.

Start to live,
learn to give,
and protect your kids.
They didn't ask to
come here.

Lord,
now I see,
it's not all about me.

In Jesus, I'm rich,
love is mine
and right within reach!

Your Word

Who do I run to
when I want to know the truth?
Your Word is a lamp to my feet.

I used to grab the phone,
now I come before your throne.
The boys just don't know,
I see where to go.
Today, my heart is strong,
I have a new home.

Money can't ruin me;
I have true prosperity.
I'm not searching for love;
mine comes from above.
I'm running in front,
isn't that something?

When they call me with questions,
I open the Good Book.
Who do I run to?
You, Lord.
Your Word is a lamp to my feet.

Keep Me

I was drowning in shame,
got tired of the game,
can't do this no more,
I'm done keeping score.

I stopped drinking;
I was just sinking.
It blocked my thinking,
and I left stinking!

What's up with the clubs
going home with lugs
and blowing cash on drugs?
I can't hang with thugs,
then risk getting mugged.

Hey, I can't do this no more.
It's become a bore.
Mama was right,
I see the light.
She said, boy, go to school,
follow the rules.

I don't need this mess,
you are not my dealer,
you won't steal my soul.
Be REAL!

I know you got a nice BOD,
but hands-off, baby.
You're a little late …
I'm sold on God.

I'm out of the streets
and through with this heat.
My Lord is Jesus,
and I know
He'll *never* leave me.

Hey, young man,
don't land in the can.
A real leader
don't have to beat her.

Wake up, brothers,
we ain't just lovers.
Use your intelligence…
our lives are relevant.

There's just one real need
that I see,
that's for His Holy Spirit
to *keep me*.

Healed

I'm no longer angry,
by His Spirit, I see
God sent His Word and
healed me.

I love my brothers,
and look up to my fathers.
I pray for those
who did me wrong.

I no longer lie
and kissed deception
goodbye.
I'm promoting unity
in my community.

It ain't no thang,
don't do gangs.
I know who I am,
more than a mere man.
I'm here for my family;
they rely on me.

Take away the booze,
I'm not here to lose.
I pulled up my pants,
and my career is scaling up!

I'm free from hate
and dead-end dates.
Jesus took all pain, anger,
disappointment, hatred, and rage
into *His body* on that tree.
God sent His Word and healed me.

Now, I'm dead to sin
and alive to righteousness!
By His stripes,
I was healed!

My Treasure

I love the One
who gave His Son.
The Lord is my treasure,
my deepest pleasure.

Yes, money is a must,
but in God, I trust,
and this is forever.

Bling is a liar,
Jesus took me higher.
He made me better.
His Spirit let me see,
He's right next to me,
my deepest pleasure.

I'm so filled with joy,
no need for toy boys.
He got me together.
My Father needs me,
and He'll never leave me,
and this is forever.

When life looks dim,
I look to Him,
my divine propeller.
The world is in a hurry,
but Jesus says, "Don't worry,
we're doing this together."

Brother, seek His face.
There's no girl to take His place.
He keeps us together.

The world left my heart homeless,
but He declared that
I'm His very BEST,
His deepest pleasure.

God is a true friend,
can I get an Amen?
The Lord is our treasure;
we're together forever.

The Kingdom

It's not just money
and being seen,
fast cars
and hanging in bars.
Unity, dignity, and prosperity ...
that's the Kingdom of God.

Everything you own
is on your back.
Can't you see,
something is wrong with that?

Lord, give me hope,
I'm tired of dope.
I'm going back to school,
I'm done acting like a fool.

Jesus said,
"One day, I'll be back."
He promised it, Jack.
We're not riding high
idolizing some brother
who's dealing crack.

Do you know who you are?
It's not about your Maserati.
What did you want to be?
You can tell me.

One by one,
God's calling us back.
The train derailed,
but it's back on track.

Love your brother
while there's still time.
Live an honorable life,
run from crime.

Stop lying to women,
as if it's a game.
You got kids out there,
who don't know your name.
Unity, dignity, and prosperity…
that's the Kingdom of God.

Purpose

I'm a man,
defined by character,
not charisma.
What are we here for?
Without God's love,
there's nothing to live for!

I'm determined to live,
I'm honored to give,
I'm not afraid to love,
my confidence is from above.

Don't sell me sex,
I demand respect.
Don't need that fix
if we can't commit.

Keep your drugs,
I ain't no thug.
I gotta life
and don't need no strife.

I'm not mad
or sad.
I forgive you, bro,
gotta go.

Getting high,
ain't fly.
Wake up, man,
it's just a lie.

I'm not into greed,
cause I'm not in need.
Is our lack driven by slack?
Think about that.
We can pay our way.
It's a brand new day.

Love with feeling.
Stop the killing.
Stop the dealing.
Let's start healing.

Words have life,
don't sink to profanity,
walk in wisdom,
guard your sanity.

Brother, honor your mother,
there's not another.
Dump the drama
and respect the baby's mama.

Provide for your children,
cause every baby boy
brings untold joy.
And every little girl
changes the world.

I am determined to be
a good example.
They look up to me
as a man of character,
and that's the key.

I'm a provider,
not a liar.
I'm not afraid
to tell the truth,
cause I ain't *scared* of you.

What are we here for?
Without God's love,
there's nothing to live for!

I Belong

I didn't falter,
I *ran* to the altar.
I know I belong to Jesus!

Dumping every addiction,
I renounce these afflictions.
I'm through running,
I've committed to becoming.

Don't go near gin,
I'm through with sin.

Lord, send a good girl,
one of your pearls.
I'm baptized and free,
the Kingdom is in me.

The Lord washed me clean.
I'm no longer mean.
It's not just us,
life has a purpose.

I'm friends with sisters,
they no longer fear us.
I pray for lost jerks
who refuse honest work.

No more unwed mothers,
I'm not that brother.
I put down chasing women,
mooching, and pimping.

Stepping out as a leader,
an *honest* woman,
I need her.
God gave me the ability
to walk in humility.
That's how I know,
I belong to Jesus!

About the Author

Gail Marie King, MA, is an author, speaker, and mentor called to ministry in 2009. She has earned a bachelor's degree in Counseling Psychology and a master's degree in Guidance and Counseling. Gail resides in Chicago, Illinois, with her loving family.

Other Books by Gail Marie King
Available in Kindle or Print

Divine Healing: All Things Are Possible
Crush Anxiety, Fear & Pain: Keys to Healing
Marry A Man Who Loves God and Adores You
Is He The One: Be Guided by God In Love
21 Insights I Wish Mom Taught Me
In Hindsight: Words of Wisdom In Quotes

*See Amazon Author Page — **Gail Marie King**, for a current list of all published titles. If any of our books have blessed you, please leave your review on Amazon. Thank you and God bless you!*

www.ingramcontent.com/pod-product-compliance
Lightning Source LLC
Chambersburg PA
CBHW070800050426
42452CB00012B/2414